The Art of Quitting

The Art of Quitting

When Enough Is Enough

Evan Harris

Illustrations by Meredith Hamilton

An EYE book

Published in 2004 for the United States and Canada by Barron’s Educational Series, Inc.

All inquiries should be addressed to:
Barron's Educational Series, Inc.
250 Wireless Boulevard
Hauppauge, New York 11788
http: //www.barronseduc.com

First published in paperback in 1996 by Fireside, a division of Simon & Schuster Inc.

M 10 9 8 7 6 5 4 3 2 1

ISBN 0-7641-2961-9

Library of Congress Control Number: 2004100207

Conceived, designed and produced by
EYE
276 Fifth Avenue
Suite 205
New York, NY 10001

Illustrations by Meredith Hamilton
Editorial and Art Direction: Michael Driscoll
Cover and Interior Design: Sheila Hart Design, Inc.

Publisher: William Kiester

Printed in China.

FOR VIC

CONTENTS

Quitting: An Introduction 8

Types, Technique, and Style: The Cornerstones of the Quit . . 12

Quitting Euphoria and Postquitting Depression 24

Technique #1: Make a Scene 31

On Inspiration, Influences, and Catalysts 32

Technique #2: Change Horses Midstream 39

Allusion and Reference 40

Technique #3: Quit Bit by Bit .45

Technique #4: Be Reasonable 47

Strategies for the Nonquitter
and for Those Who Have Been Quit 48

Technique #5: Achieve and Vanish 55

Every Disappearance Is a Possible Quit 56

Technique #6: Fail and Disappear 61

The Bet Hedge 62

Technique #7: Muster Willpower 66

Retroactive Quitting: Myth or Reality? 68

Technique #8: Be Passive-Aggressive 73

Technique #9: Get Fed Up 74

Private Quitting 76

Technique #10: Quit in the Clutch 81

The Principled Quit 83
Technique #11: Repudiate Your Ideas 87
Quitting Before Beginning
and Quitting While You Are Ahead 88
Technique #12: Abandon and Conceal 93
Technique #13: Take Revenge 94
The Requit 96
Technique #14: Burn a Bridge .101
Technique #15: Sulk 103
The Unquit and Quitting the Quit: A Discussion 104
Technique #16: Plot and Endure 109
On the Lingering Quit 110
Technique #17: Deny Involvement 115
On Quitting an Obsession 116
Technique #18: Give Up 122
Quitting the Search for Happiness 124
Technique #19: Take to Your Bed 129
The Painful Quit and the Ill-Fated Quit:
A Comparative Study 130
Technique #20: Wipe the Slate Clean 137
Consider the Quit 138

Quitting: An Introduction

The option of quitting has long been undervalued and underused. Advice like "Put your nose to the grindstone" and "Give it time" has all but supplanted the wisdom of frustration and impetuosity. The more-responsible-than-thou, more-ambitious-than-thou, tougher-than-thou attitude of antiquitters intimidates potential quitters into shying away from risk and proceeding with the status quo.

The cozy, smug security of the antiquitter is to be avoided at all costs. Quitters must not be frightened by the potentially cataclysmic outcome of a particular quit. Disaster beats stasis—better to be a rolling stone than a moss-covered rock. Furthermore, the results of a quit must never eclipse the joy, beauty, and pleasure (even if it be perverse) of the quit itself. A well-executed quit is its own reward.

There is nothing like the independence of the quitter, driven by a volition of her very own. She doesn't jump off the cliff just because everyone else is doing it; she doesn't keep herself from jumping just because everyone else is afraid to try. The quitter is a star in the universe of decision making. The quitter takes her chances. The quitter decides for herself when enough is enough.

Quitting does not come out of the clear blue sky. Every quitter enters into his quit armed with something to quit, a number of methods at his disposal, and a natural predilection for how to proceed. Type of quit, technique, and style of the quitter are the three components that go into every quit, from the monumental to the insignificant, the enviable to the absurd. The combination of these elements gives rise to the quit, and even though there are only three variables, no two quits are exactly alike. You and your friend next door may both quit shoveling the walk in the wintertime, but you will never quit it in exactly the same way. The spin on your technique will be subtly distinct; you will quit with a similar but slightly different style. Details count. The minutiae are crucial.

No matter what, the quitter has his work cut out for him. There are lots of elements to keep track of as you go on with your work, even if quitting is a labor of love. First and foremost, you must be aware of the myriad possibilities that exist in each element of the quit.

Types of Quits

Survey the landscape. Take a look around. You live in a world composed of things that can be quit. The potential for quitting lurks and presents itself at every turn. For the purposes of discussion, quitting can be broken down into categories, or fields.

The following is a list of broad quitting fields:

1. *Job Quitting.* Quitting any labor, paid or unpaid.

2. *Person Quitting.* Quitting seeing, talking to, liking, listening to, writing to, telephoning, admiring, tolerating, wishing well, caring for, banking on, being amused by, being changed by, or loving any person or group of people.

3. *Thing Quitting.* The quitting of inanimate objects, food products, and anything animal (except people), vegetable, or mineral.

4. *Location Quitting.* Quitting a city, town, country, etcetera. Not the same as moving.*

*All location quits are moves, but not all moves are location quits. The location quit does not necessarily have anything to do with the actual place the quitter goes, but it has everything to do with the place the quitter has left behind.

The location quit is marked by a driving need to get away, disgust at one's present living arrangements, and an overwhelming sense of place-related discomfort. It can be spurred on by many things, from a messy break-up to ill health. Sometimes the location quit is attended by a desire to see new things or experience new places, but not always, by any means. The location quit is about leaving, not arriving.

The Possibilities Are Endless

5. *Idea Quitting.* Stopping adhering to or eschewing any idea, system of ideas, thought, psychological condition, or emotional state.†

6. *Habit Quitting.* Eradicating the doing of something that you engage in as a matter of course on a regular basis. Generally involves quitting things that are destructive or bad for your health.§

The above fields describe the raw materials of quitting upon which the quitter practices her art. An understanding of the basic quitting fields can help the quitter focus in on what it is precisely that she doesn't want. Knowledge is power. Know your quits.

†Once you start to tangle with the notion of quitting fields (job, person, thing, location, idea, habit), you can't help but consider a very disturbing question: Is all quitting reducible to idea quitting? Is becoming a vegetarian a thing quit, or is it really an idea quit? Say you quit mopping your floor. Are you quitting a thing—your mop—or are you quitting an idea: that everyone should have a clean floor?

If every quit is an idea quit, why bother with distinctions? Why not admit that there is only one type of quit, and call all the other categories manifestations of the idea quit?

Ignore this unsettling notion. It is too overwhelming. The reality is that when it comes to quitting, you must divide and conquer. Focus in. Bother with distinctions. The actual material of a quit—the person, place, job, or thing that must be gotten rid of—indicates what the quitter is having ideas about. Pretend that the manifestations of your ideas are as important as the ideas themselves. Never mind that quitting is, at bottom, all in your mind.

§Habits should be quit with caution. It is a bad idea to quit with an eye on outcome alone, because this gives short shrift to the pleasure derived from quitting itself. Habit quitting is no walk in the park and often hinges on being deprived of pleasure. Even if what you are quitting is bad for you, too much habit quitting will forge an association between being deprived and quitting. All unpleasant associations with quitting should be kept to an absolute minimum.

Quitting Technique

Like all arts, quitting requires skill. Like all skills, skill in quitting requires technique. Most quitters begin with a measure of native talent, but even so, the quitter needs working methods.

The development and perfection of quitting technique is a dual process. First, the quitter must identify sound and creative methods to meet his quitting needs. Second, the quitter must practice. Practicing often comes more easily to the quitter than developing methods to do so. Although quitters quit by nature, they often have trouble using a range of methods and varying the method to best execute the quit. Quitters, like everyone else, get mired in the status quo, reluctant to deviate from their usual style or method of procedure. Be brave. Dream up a new technique. Go out into the world in search of a testing ground.

Quitting is an exercise in creativity. The more quitting techniques, the smarter the quitter. The smarter the quitter, the better the quit. The better the quit, the better the quitter.

The actual number of quitting techniques available to the quitter cannot be guessed at. An exhaustive list of techniques could not be drawn up by even the most diligent quitter with a lot of time on his hands, interested in exploring all of his options.

The world of quitting technique is not only large but expanding. All manner of cutting and pasting and patchwork goes on as quitters proceed with their work. Old techniques are modified and new techniques are created to meet the needs of the quit in question. There are standby techniques that have been around since the dawn of time, and techniques so revolutionary they have been tested by only the most cutting-edge quitters.

The quitter does not have to use every technique he comes in contact with right away. He can hoard it and use it later, cannibalize it for parts, or use it in conjunction with another method. The important thing is to be broad-minded and to consider the gleaning of technique part of your work as a quitter. Notice quitting methods in the pages of history and literature. Cull them from overheard conversations. Make them up out of your head. Once you amass a stockpile of techniques, you are in a position to choose among them.

A word of caution: Don't just pick the first technique that crawls out from the woodwork. Every technique does not make a good marriage with every type of quit. Sometimes the technique you feel the most affinity for, the one you are convinced best expresses your quitting style and personality, just won't work for the type of quit you need to execute. If the Bridge Burn lies close to your heart and you wish you could use it all the time, but you are attempting a habit quit, you're out of luck. To Bridge Burn successfully, going back has to be totally impossible; you have to ostracize yourself completely. Unfortunately, the habit doesn't care if you quit. The nails don't notice if you stop biting them: They have no feelings, do not check up on references, and do not keep a permanent record of your actions. Likewise, Taking Revenge and Making a Scene just do not make sense when it is a habit that you are planning to quit.

Or say you want to quit an idea, like the belief in reincarnation. Don't use the Take to Your Bed technique. Picture it: There you are in bed. What better place to spend time wondering if you aren't a Victorian lady reincarnated?

Occasionally, it will be crystal clear which technique you need to use for a particular quit. Sometimes, in fact, you will dispatch the whole quit without consciously picking a method at all. Sometimes you don't have time. Sometimes you don't have control. Eleventh-hour quits just happen; Giving Up is often an impulse divorced from rational processes of thought. The Piecemeal Quit tends to creep up on you; the Passive-Aggressive Quit is often well under way by the time you realize you are quitting.

Remember, you can always abandon ship and pick a new technique. Sulk until you can think of a better course of action. Abandon and Conceal to keep your finger in the quitting pie. Use one technique to catapult you to the next. Get fancy. Change Horses Midstream as often as you choose.

The use of certain techniques often inspires the use of others. If your strategy is to use the Plot and Endure to execute a difficult location quit, don't be surprised if you are so pent and stifled by the end of it that you Make a Huge Scene. If you abandon all sense of decorum at the end of a love affair and

Take Revenge in a fit of pique, do not be alarmed if you soon find yourself Taking to Your Bed out of sheer exhaustion.

Above all, the quitter should be creative and try as many different techniques as possible. This is how quitting has survived and triumphed through history. There is always something new under the quitting sun—get to it by dint of tireless tinkering and testing. Improve yourself. Quit and keep on quitting.

Quitting Style

Technique is, to a certain extent, a vehicle for style. The quitter's particular quitting style allows her to claim a technique and mold it to fit the dimensions of the quit at hand. Style is the texture of action, the timbre of decision making, the feel and flavor of volition.

Some quitters are born with style—every quit these lucky quitters accomplish is illuminated with the glow of finesse. Most quitters, though, find it necessary to develop their quitting style as their career progresses and their views on quitting solidify.

The notion of style depends on the notion of individuality, and there are as many quitting styles as there are quitters. An individual's quitting style generally reflects the individual's personality: Reckless people will quit in a headlong rush; rational people will quit with a list in hand. Humble people will quit with humility; proud people will quit with pride, if not hubris. However, in some instances the execution of a quit brings out less dominant, and even latent, aspects of the quitter's personality. Aggressive people suddenly lose their bite, throw up their hands, and give up without a fight. Composed people fly off the handle, lose their cool, and run screaming for the hills. Meticulous people stop caring about details, forget about covering bases, and abandon ship.

All quitters should allow themselves to succumb to the influence of the quit itself. The quit may demand drama from an introvert, prudence from an inveterate risk taker, impatience from a person who would normally be willing to wait forever. Though the quit can give rise to qualities heretofore unnoticed, unrecognized, or unsung, the quitter should nonetheless quit in keeping with her personality. Complete departure from your basic nature will engender postquitting shame, doubt, and quitting denial. You will look back on the quit and be embarrassed that you ever acted that way, unable to believe you ever said that and ultimately forced to deny it was you who even executed the quit.

•

The three essential elements that go into each quit—quitting field, quitting technique, and quitting style—create the face of a particular quitter's career. Without knowledge of the quitting fields, the quitter will be unable to isolate—among the overwhelming cacophony of possibilities—exactly what to quit. Without technique, the quitter will find herself stumbling blindly, unable to execute an artful quit. Without style, the quitter will just be going through the motions. Don't fail to fulfill your potential as a quitter. Make a name for yourself. Even quitters unburdened by troublesome fame complexes should be loath to see their quitting toil go to waste.

Armed with an understanding of the three crucial components of the quit, the quitter can embark on a long and fruitful life graced and driven by quitting. Pick your raw material; marshal your techniques; summon the elements of your quitting style. Quit the next thing that comes your way.

Quitting Euphoria and Postquitting Depression

Most quitting conforms to a loose schedule. Various stages lead up to the quit; these differ in length and import for each quitter, but most experience them at some point in some form. First, the quitter thinks about quitting. This stage includes contemplating unhappiness, frustration, and shame, and dwelling on discomforts, injustices, and boredom. It can satisfy the quitter for months or even years. Next the

The Quit

quitter fantasizes about methods of quitting. This stage is often the most creative part of the process, and many quitters draw it out, letting the imaginative quality inherent in the quitter come to the fore. Then the quitter picks a method and homes in on its execution. Finally, the quitter quits.

Many quitters experience an exhilaration attendant upon quitting, known as quitting euphoria. Quitting euphoria can be likened to the feeling of being in love, except that the quitter is in love with his decision. Solipsism has its benefits.

Unfortunately, the euphoria eventually fades. Some quitters cope with this eventuality better than others. Some have a very hard time of it indeed, and the postquit period can be a trying time. Postquit exhaustion, depression, and feelings of worthlessness should be considered an occupational hazard. Although these feelings are daunting, if handled correctly they will destroy neither the

The Euphoria

quitter's facility and native talent for quitting nor the impulse to quit again.

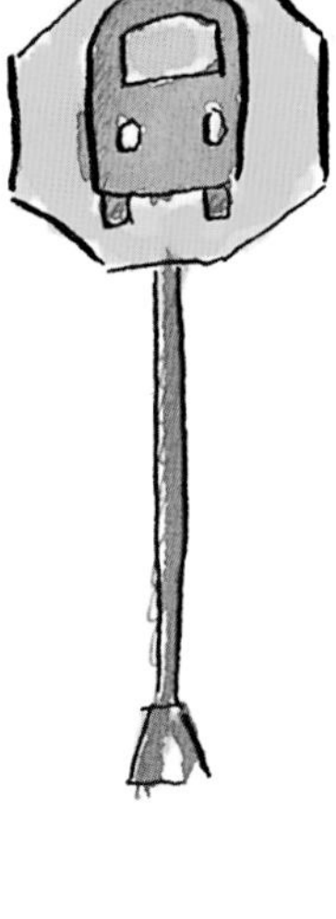

The Depression

The following are some strategies for combating postquitting lassitude and depression:

1. Tell everyone you know that you have quit. Because of the stigma attached to it, many quitters deny themselves the pride and gratification of quitting. Pick someone you know will disapprove of your quit and bludgeon him with every detail. Pick someone you know will approve and let him congratulate you. If everyone you know already knows that you quit, tell them again. Send announcements in the mail, make phone calls, invite people to your house for dinner, and dwell on your quit all evening. Make everyone discuss it until you rally.

2. Think about quitting something else. This will reacquaint you with the process. For the sake of clarity, think about quitting something you like and have no intention of quitting: If you're

madly in love, think about leaving; if you live in a beautiful house, think about moving; if you're reading a great book, think about putting it down. Thinking about quitting will remind you of how motivating the beginning stages of the quitting process are, and will eventually spur you on to quit again.

3. Attach yourself to someone else's quit. If you are suffering from postquitting ennui, latching on to someone else's quit can be quite gratifying. Immerse yourself in the details. Become obsessed with the blow by blow. Siphon off as much of your subject's quitting euphoria as possible.

4. Dwell on what a drag things were before you quit. Congratulate yourself on your exemplary ability to make difficult decisions and your rare capacity for volition. Become convinced that you've taken the first step in piloting your destiny. Shore up your suffering ego. Put wind in the sails of your flagging self-esteem. Pat yourself on the back until you feel better.

5. Suffer. Be really sad. Cry in your beer and cash in on all the credit you have with friends by going on and on about how unhappy you are, and what a disaster your life has become. Immerse yourself; become a basket case; spiral. Eventually, you will become bored with being unhappy, or simply bored with yourself. Old dissatisfaction with your life will become subsumed by a new inability to tolerate your mental state. New quitting possibilities will come out of the woodwork.

6. Replay your quit in the screening room of your consciousness. Watch it over and over, and be very critical. Beat yourself up over your failure to take time and savor the joy of quitting or, conversely, your failure to cut to the chase and experience the full impact of your quit. Wish you had said better, smarter, more cinematic things. Wish you had been more decisive, paid more attention to detail, or been better prepared for the

curve ball. Obsess on the graceless way you left the room or signed the letter or framed the argument. Hate what you were wearing. Vow to be less of a dork next time, and start planning the execution of a more attractive quit.

Replay your quit in the screening room of your consciousness.

TECHNIQUE # 1

Make a Scene

Create drama or high tension. Walk into the Department of Motor Vehicles and announce to the long line of people there that you will no longer be registering your car; be loud; tear up your registration certificate.

Choose a location at work with maximum visibility and good acoustics. Lie in wait for your boss to enrage you one too many times; respond by tearing up important documents and throwing things. Leave, shouting threats.

Stand outside your boyfriend's door screaming insults and obscenities. Refuse to leave. Make his neighbors wonder why he is such a jerk. Make him wish he had never been born.

On Inspiration, Influences, and Catalysts

When it comes down to it, quitting is a solitary affair. You're in it by yourself. You can't elect a proxy; you can't split the tab. However, before the moment of the quit, the quitter is faced with a world full of advice, signs, role models, and extenuating circumstances that can and do affect the quit. You run up against other people. They tell you things. You notice various coincidences and telling events. They give you ideas.

The major categories of elements that inspire, influence, and act as catalysts for quitting are as follows:

1. *Other People's Quits.* Other people act as role models, both positive and negative, for quitting. Deciding to renounce the cage of a middle-class existence for the free and easy artist's life in Tahiti, like Paul Gauguin, is an example of a positive use of someone else's quit. Wanting to be brilliant and then dropping out of sight, like J.D. Salinger, can be considered taking inspiration from a member of the quitter hall of fame. Feeling scared that if you don't quit, you're going to

Quitting Hall of Fame

Paul Gaugin

end up like such and such relentless person who spent his whole life beating a dead horse, and quitting to avoid that fate is paying attention to a warning.

(2) *Other People Egging You On.* Other people can help precipitate a quit in a number of ways, which include sympathetic listening, giving advice, being supportive, offering suggestions, and generally adding fuel to the fire. Comments like "If I were you, I wouldn't give notice at all," "Of course you don't have to go through with it," and "It is your human right to quit" are among the proquitting sentiments other people provide. The people who supply this kind of support are often helpful in the postquitting period as well.

(3) *Signs.* If you dream that you quit your job and the whole place fell apart and all your complaints and feelings of not being appreciated were vindicated, it is a sign that you should quit your job. If you go to register for classes at the school you are attending and every one you were pretending to want to take is full, it is a sign that you should quit school. If the person you are dating cannot communicate and does not understand you, and his telephone goes on the fritz so that there's a lot of static and you can't hear each other talking, it is a sign that you should quit that person. If you open up a magazine and randomly turn to a page with a story about the adverse effects of birth-control pills, it is a sign to quit taking them.

The world is practically sinking under the weight of signs that prefigure and indicate the suspiciousness of various quits. Keep your eyes open.

4. *Safety Nets.* Safety nets often allow quitters to go ahead without fear, and thus act as quitting catalysts. A love interest waiting in the wings, an inheritance, a dangling job offer—all are safety nets that make the quitter feel he will not drop into the void if he quits. Safety net quitting isn't the bravest thing in the world, but it beats not quitting at all. It should be noted that there is a fine line between safety net quitting and the bet hedge (see p. 62); this line has to be watched carefully by each individual quitter. If the safety net seems to have dropped out of the sky into the quitter's lap, it is sometimes interpreted as a sign.

5. *Last Straws.* Last straws indicate the point at which the quitter decides enough is enough. Your boyfriend ignores your birthday. You quit him. Eating a bowl of beet soup finally makes you throw up.

The Last Straw

You quit eating it. Your landlord refuses to fix the leak in the bathroom of the apartment above yours, and a chunk of the ceiling falls in. You quit paying rent.

6. *Literature and Music.* Quitting has been used as the subject matter for many creative productions. Books such as *The Tin Drum* (the main character, Oscar, willfully quits growing at the age of three), the *Iliad* (Achilles quits fighting in the Trojan War, then returns, quitting his quit), and *Germinal* (coal miners quit working and go on strike) are part of the canon of quitting literature, and inspire new and seasoned quitters alike. Art is supposed to be inspiring and change people's lives. Take advantage.

   Songs like "It Ain't Me, Babe," "These Boots Were Made for Walkin'," "Return to Sender," and "Fifty Ways to Leave Your Lover" describe proquitting sentiment and promote inspiring quitting messages. When they come on the radio, turn it up.

The inspiration, influences, and catalysts for quitting are subjective and serve as reflections of each quitter's consciousness. A definite sign for one quitter is merely a coincidence for another; the last straw for one quitter is just the beginning of the end for the next.

Different quitters are inspired by different catalysts: Your sister's constant refrain that you should quit your city goes in one ear and out the other, but finding a piece of mail in your mailbox addressed to someone else suddenly makes you realize that you have to flee. You ignore the fact that your rent has gone up—for some, a classic last straw—but reading F. Scott Fitzgerald and admiring his expatriate life puts you on the bus to execute a location quit of romantic, sweeping dimension.

TECHNIQUE #2

Change Horses Midstream

Don't be intimidated by antiquitter fixation on consistency and diligence. Don't worry about seeing things through or staying with your original plan. Changing horses midstream is perfectly okay. Do it at the drop of a hat. Labor to become the executive director of a national organization, then quit to have a baby and be a full-time mom. Get into college on a football scholarship. Arrive, refuse to play, and become the editor of the school newspaper. Take your inspiration from Grace Kelly, who quit being a movie star to become a princess. For a multifaceted look at horse changing, study the career of Bob Dylan, who went from acoustic to electric on his guitar and secular to devout in his spiritual life.

Allusion and Reference

Every person is a potential quitter; every activity is a potential quit. A stunning amount of quitting goes on in the world, and it can be difficult for an individual quitter to tell where her quits fall in the grand scheme of things, and how best to respond to the work of other quitters.

Your particular quits are part of a long tradition of quitting, which should be respected, learned from, and admired. You must also recognize that quits differ in weight. Your decision to quit your city for a location cure is not the same as the Jews' exodus from Egypt. Your refusing to sing "Happy Birthday" at family gatherings is not the same as Cat Stevens refusing to make any more records and leaving fame behind.

It is only human to want to place all things in a hierarchical order, and perhaps this accounts for a general tendency to privilege some quits above others. This is a good instinct. All things are not the same as all other things.

Martin Luther quit crucial tenets of the Catholic church; the face of Europe was changed. Thomas Jefferson and the signers of the Declaration of Independence quit the tyranny of King George; a nation was born. Galileo quit believing the sun revolved around the Earth; the age of enlightenment began. Certain quits are important not only for their skill of execution but also for their scope.

Assigning weight to a quit is not a matter of judging it good or bad. No quit is silly on account of content alone. In the hands of an accomplished quitter, the decision to stop flushing the toilet might be a thing of beauty. Similarly, a cloddish quitter can render a universally regarded quit, such as a defection or an abdication of the throne, ridiculous.

Don't worry too much about how other quitters have gone about things. Too much analysis of the whats and hows and whens and whys of important quits will make you crazy. You can never precisely replicate another quitter's world-class quit; trying only makes you a copycat. However, a little emulation never hurts a developing quitter. It's perfectly okay to follow in the footsteps of a favorite quitter (famous or not), borrowing technique and the broad strokes of style. This is part of the process of understanding the dimensions and importance of your own quits and defining your role in the world of quitting.

Naturally, emulation brings up the question of allusion and reference. Some quits are in the public domain; these can and should be quoted freely. For example, any and all serial divorcing of wives is a clear reference to Henry VIII. The extent to which you capitalize on the irony or historical implications of this is up to you.

More obscure quits—and the quitter to whom they are attached—should be cited. If you quit reading the newspaper because your friend Andy did, and you think it was an important statement about information overload and the inability of the mass media to accurately report the truth, you should cite him and it as such. The same goes for changing your name because you want to be just like Harry Houdini or Judy Garland, both relatively unsung name quitters who were famous for other accomplishments. Each quitter must take on the responsibility of citation. Crediting the quit or quitter to whom you are referring not only helps to clarify your own quitting style and intentions, but also highlights the quitting way, celebrating its history of great minds and great moments.

The quits that an inspiring quitter executes should be considered that quitter's gift to the world of quitting. Admiring quitters can feel free to explore the technique and plumb it for whatever possibilities it may hold.

Don't be sad if you don't get attention or praise for your quits. Remember, many important quitters are not recognized until they are long gone. The weight of the quit kicks in with time. Quitters die paupers. Quitters publish posthumously. Quitters are vindicated centuries later. Quit what you must, and quit in your own way, but always see yourself as part of the larger world of quitting.

TECHNIQUE #3

Quit Bit by Bit

This method, also known as the Piecemeal Quit, describes a group of related quits executed one after another. Each quit in the series limbers you up, and together they form the big quit. The Piecemeal Quit allows you to gradually eliminate things from your life and is generally designed to help you accomplish a quit that is too overreaching to manage all at once. The Piecemeal Quit creates momentum as it unfolds, and is thus well suited for use in quitting large or unwieldy things.

If you are overwhelmed at the prospect of leaving your job, work yourself up to it. Quit making work-related telephone calls. Quit returning work-related telephone calls. Become impossible to get in touch with while actually in the workplace. Stop keeping your desk or workstation tidy. Stop doing your

DAY ONE

DAY TWO

WORK WELL. STOP DOING YOUR WORK AT ALL. QUIT YOUR JOB.

IF YOU NEED TO WARM UP FOR A LOCATION QUIT, GET YOURSELF USED TO IT LITTLE BY LITTLE. QUIT CHECKING THE WEATHER REPORT FOR YOUR CITY OR TOWN. QUIT READING THE LOCAL NEWSPAPER. QUIT VOTING IN LOCAL ELECTIONS. STOP WRITING YOUR RETURN ADDRESS ON CORRESPONDENCE. QUIT TELLING PEOPLE WHERE YOU LIVE. QUIT SPENDING TIME AT HOME. MOVE.

IF YOU CAN'T GET IT TOGETHER TO QUIT YOUR HUSBAND IN ONE FELL SWOOP, DO IT ONE STEP AT A TIME. QUIT USING YOUR HUSBAND'S LAST NAME. QUIT REFERRING TO HIM AS YOUR HUSBAND. STOP SLEEPING IN THE SAME BED. STOP WEARING YOUR WEDDING RING. FILE FOR DIVORCE.

DAY THREE

TECHNIQUE #4

Be Reasonable

CALMLY OUTLINE ALL THE REASONS YOU SHOULD QUIT WHATEVER ACTIVITY IS COMING UP ON YOUR QUITTING SCREEN. CHECK TO MAKE SURE YOU'RE NOT DELUDING YOURSELF, RATIONALIZING, OR IN ANY WAY PULLING THE WOOL OVER YOUR EYES. BE REALLY GROWN-UP ABOUT THE WHOLE THING.

IF YOU ARE QUITTING YOUR JOB, WRITE A DETAILED LETTER EXPLAINING THE REASONS WHY; ARRANGE A MEETING WITH YOUR BOSS TO DELIVER AND DISCUSS THE NEWS; GIVE AN APPROPRIATE AMOUNT OF NOTICE AND WORK DILIGENTLY THROUGH THE TIME TO WHICH YOU HAVE COMMITTED YOURSELF. IF YOU ARE QUITTING YOUR BOYFRIEND, SIT DOWN AND EXPLAIN REASONABLY THAT YOU ARE NO LONGER HIS GIRLFRIEND. DO NOT SCREAM AND YELL. SAY YOU STILL WANT TO BE FRIENDS.

THE BE REASONABLE TECHNIQUE IS GOOD FOR THE BEGINNER WHO HAS NOT YET ESTABLISHED HIS OWN QUITTING STYLE. IT IS ALSO USEFUL FOR THE INSECURE QUITTER, BECAUSE IT ERADICATES FEARS OF SEEMING FLAKY OR CHILDISH. BE REASONABLE IS A BARE-BONES TECHNIQUE. IF YOU CAN MANAGE TO PULL YOURSELF TOGETHER AND SPEAK IN COHERENT SENTENCES FOR, SAY, A HALF-HOUR, YOU CAN CARRY IT OFF.

Strategies for the Nonquitter and for Those Who Have Been Quit

Not everyone was born to quit. Still, some nonquitters are friends of the quitting way. They embrace quitting in theory but have different things to do when it comes around to practice. They stick it out, they cling, they hold the fort. They keep the old flag flying, settle in, wait and see.

Nonquitters with proquitter sentiments and an allegiance, albeit theoretical, to the quitting way sometimes feel alienated. This unpleasantness can be avoided; the sympathetic nonquitter can undertake plenty of activities. The following are some options for supporting the quitting way without actually quitting:

1. Organize an event to champion, promote, or encourage your favorite quitting activity or quitter. Do not be intimidated by large-scale campaigns like the Great American Smoke-Out. You may not get huge, mainstream approval for your event, but that doesn't mean nobody cares.

Hold a banquet honoring the quitters in your community. Organize a panel discussion or symposium on issues in quitting at your local Y. Make posters celebrating the history of quitting. Hang the posters all over the place.

2. Send anonymous letters to people you think should be quitting that say things like "Get out while you can," "Turn in your badge," and "Jump ship." Let them know someone is keeping tabs.

3. Write a letter to the editor of your local newspaper spotlighting a current or controversial issue in quitting. Be prepared to defend yourself against rebuttals from antiquitters.

4. Talk about all the people you know who are boycotting things. Sigh and say you think it's great.

5. If you are in business, adjust management practices to include a policy on quitters. Hire a quitter; promote a quitter; transfer a quitter to the personnel department.

6. Contact your senator or congressperson. Urge her to protect the rights of quitters.

7. Never cross picket lines.

8. Tout quitters as role models for your children. Fill their shelves with books written by quitters: Start with Salinger; up the ante with Rimbaud. Take your children to see movies starring A-list quitters like Grace Kelly and Greta Garbo. Make the figures in American history come alive by filling your children in on their quits: George Washington declined a

third term as president, setting the standard for the great American tradition of quitting while ahead; Rosa Parks quit sitting in the back of the bus, executing a landmark principled quit. Point out that the Twenty-first Amendment to the Constitution was America's quit of prohibition. Make sure your kids know the exact date America quit the gold standard, and make them aware that America is a melting pot of location quitters. When your child's teacher assigns an oral report on a famous person, suggest a quitter.

9. Give sanctuary to a quitter. Be a stop on the underground railroad for quitters on the run. Lie and say you have never heard of the quitter when pressed by her pursuers. Give false information to throw them off the track.

In addition to sympathetic nonquitters, people who are being quit are in a position to support the quitting way. Although people in this situation are rarely very enthusiastic about quitting, it is important for them to separate the emotional pain of the specific quit that is being perpetrated on them from the quitting way as a whole. Following are some options:

1. Challenge the person who is quitting you. Give off a lot of static, and call her method into question. If she is employing the Passive-Aggressive technique, point out how much more effective Making a Scene would be. If she is Bridge Burning, refuse to be alienated. If she is Giving Up, draw her into a long discussion on why she should have quit while she was ahead instead. If she is trying to quit while she's ahead, seduce her into a lingering quit. Help the quitter develop and perfect her quitting technique by providing something to work against.

Give Sanctuary to a Quitter

2. Ponder the larger significance. See that you are a cog in the wheel of the great quitting machine that turns the world. Do not cramp the quitter's style lest you unwittingly throw off the course of history.

3. Lash out. Be impossible to get rid of. Dog the quitter's steps and refuse to stop calling. Generally resist being quit at every turn. Force the quitter to be tireless and renew her commitment to quitting you.

4. Turn around and quit something yourself. Add to the debate by joining the army of quitters, which has absolutely no requirement for admission except that you quit and keep on quitting.

TECHNIQUE #5

Achieve and Vanish

The Achieve and Vanish is extremely effective, and is high on any quitter's ambition list. The quitting that results from this technique often makes quitting history: Witness grandmaster Bobby Fisher, who quit playing chess and vanished completely from the public eye for 17 years after winning the world championship. Like all quitters who Achieve and Vanish, Fisher rendered absurd the antiquitter cliché "Quitters never win and winners never quit."

Star in an Academy Award-winning movie, and then drop out of sight. Be presented with your country's medal of honor, and then go into exile. Win the Olympic gold medal for skiing; don't do any commercials afterward, hang up your poles, and move to a tropical island, leaving no forwarding address.

Every Disappearance Is a Possible Quit

Anytime a person disappears from the public eye or the bosom of his family, or just evaporates altogether, there is a possibility that a quit has taken place. Naturally, exceptions exist. Clear cases of kidnapping don't count. But still, even with these special cases in mind, if the Bureau of Missing Persons was more willing to take quitting into account, they could clear out a few files and stop feeling so bogged down. Of course, it's hard to say how they would proceed with the file weeding. Quitters who see fit to disappear do not make themselves available for mystery solving.

The hands-down best execution of a disappearance quit was performed by D.B. Cooper, who disappeared on November 24, 1971, after completing the only successful airplane hijacking inside the continental United States. He jumped out of the plane someplace between Seattle and Reno (using one of the four parachutes he had demanded, along with a whole lot of cash), and remains at large, an acknowledged and celebrated quitter.

In most cases of disappearance, however, quitting is not even considered as a possible solution to the mystery. Authorities—and the public—are much happier to suspect foul play, as they conjure up grisly tales of burials and drownings.

Why is it that we would rather pronounce Amelia Earhart, who disappeared July 3, 1937, dead and resting at the bottom of the ocean than entertain the notion that she may have opted out of the transcontinental flight racket and quit the public eye? Why are we so sure that Joseph Crater, a New York Supreme Court justice who disappeared August 6, 1930, met no good end rather than suppose he happily quit public office via a vanishing? The judge was last seen driving away in the back of a New York City taxicab. Who's to say? Maybe the judge had just had enough.*

Jimmy Hoffa, who disappeared on July 30, 1975, was not necessarily cut up into little bits and put in a suitcase and thrown into some body of water someplace. Just because we assume he was murdered and the murder was covered up does not make it so. Perhaps he'd had it with the whole teamster/mobster way of life and wanted to start over in some small midwestern town. It is interesting to note that shortly before his disappearance, Hoffa had made this loaded statement: "The strong survive and the weak disappear. We do not propose to disappear." It is anybody's guess what he meant by this, but there might well have been some irony or a clue encoded in his speech.

* Several months after his disappearance, his wife returned from Maine, where she had been hiding from the press, to their New York City apartment. A thorough investigation was in full swing, and the entire apartment had been searched. When she arrived back home, there were financial documents in a drawer that, according to the investigators, had absolutely not been there before. Copies of a life insurance policy, bank account statements, stuff like that. The judge may well have returned to the scene of his quit to make sure his wife was financially secure. Quitters are not necessarily bad providers.

Perhaps the disappearance of the Flight 19 squadron constitutes the most powerful evidence of society's unwillingness to consider quitting as an explanation for disappearance. On December 5, 1945, six military aircraft vanished somewhere over the Atlantic Ocean in the process of trying to complete a triangle-shaped training run off the Florida coast. The evidence is all very hazy. They got lost; there were a bunch of weird radio communications. After 7:04 P.M. nothing was heard from any of the planes; neither hide nor hair was ever found. From this set of facts, we get the stew of conspiracy theories and fantasies that are labeled the Bermuda Triangle: Flight 19 was swept into a space vacuum; Flight 19 was shot down by the Russians; Flight 19 was beamed up by Martians. The possibility of supernatural occurrences, extraterrestrials, and alternate time and space configurations

Ain't dis da life...

Jimmy Hoffa Alive and Well Doing the Organic Thing in Vermont are, it seems, more plausible than the possibility of a quit. Maybe Flight 19 was sick of bombing and just kept on flying. Maybe they all decided to picnic on a tropical island, forget about the air force, and never come back.

The fact is, no body, no proof. No proof, no certainty. Where there's uncertainty, there is room for any number of explanations. Understand that the notion "vanished into thin air" is a figure of speech. The thickness or thinness of the air has nothing to do with quitting. The world is big. There's always an out. Never assume that the disappeared party isn't gone on purpose.

TECHNIQUE #6

Fail and Disappear

THIS METHOD IS SIMILAR TO THE ACHIEVE AND VANISH IN FORM, BUT THE CONTENT IS ENTIRELY DIFFERENT. INSTEAD OF PRAISE OR ADULATION, THE QUITTER MUST GARNER, IN THE PREQUITTING STAGE, DISAPPROVAL AND CONDEMNATION.

THE FAIL AND DISAPPEAR MAY SEEM TO HAVE LITTLE GLORY, AND THUS REDUCE QUITTING VALUE, BUT THIS IS NOT SO. FAILING IS BIG. FAILING IS TRAGIC. BY FOLLOWING YOUR FAILURE WITH A DISAPPEARANCE, YOU WILL HAVE AMPLE TIME TO NURSE YOUR INADEQUACY AND BECOME DISILLUSIONED. THESE FEELINGS WILL SOLIDIFY THE QUIT.

WRITE A TERRIBLE BOOK THAT GETS HORRIBLE REVIEWS, SELLS PITIFULLY, AND FALLS WAY BELOW ALL THE STANDARDS YOU EVER SET FOR YOURSELF, THEN NEVER WRITE ANOTHER WORD AGAIN. LOSE A MAJOR ACCOUNT, SALE, DEAL, OR CLIENT. GO ON VACATION AND NEVER COME BACK. RUN FOR POLITICAL OFFICE AND LOSE, THEN LEAVE THE COUNTRY.

The Bet Hedge

The bet hedge, defined as "betting on both sides so as to guard against loss," is a form of self-protection. The bet hedger always covers his bases, pathologically avoiding risk. All quitting, however, involves some risk. If you leave something behind, you risk missing it; if you eradicate something from your life, you risk experiencing a great big hole where the thing once was.

Also defined as a "calculatedly noncommittal or evasive statement," the bet hedge is thoroughly cagey and dishonest. The quitting way, of course, numbers cagey and dishonest quitters in its ranks, but the confirmed bet hedger will never really embrace the quitting way. Why? Because the bet hedger's racket is to avoid making a decision at all costs. The bet hedger has her cake and eats it, too, on a regular basis. She covers up and sneaks around and drives herself crazy with the chore of keeping her various lies straight, all to escape making a painful, unpleasant, or inconvenient decision. Quitting, the grandest form of decision making, is totally contrary to the bet hedge.

The bet hedger occasionally employs a tactic known as the Fixed-Time Quit. She stops doing something for a limited period of time, reserving the option to discontinue the quit after the fixed time has elapsed. "I'm going to quit biting my nails until after

the interview" and "I'm not speaking to him until he apologizes" are common constructions.

Thus, the bet hedger quits but does not commit. To call this quitting is absurd, and underscores the bet hedger's tendency to delude herself.

No one ever said ambivalence does not figure into the psychology of the quitter: Lots of quitters are of two minds or have divided hearts. Ambivalence makes a quit difficult, but it does not prevent the true quitter from quitting. The bet hedge, an aggressive manifestation and glorification of ambivalence, is the archenemy of the quitting way.

Bet hedgers spend valuable quitting time evading all manner of risk. Bet hedgers refuse to make the decision to quit. Bet hedgers attempt to corrupt quitting by appropriating its language for their own purposes.

Bet hedgers can't even get a day pass into quitting heaven.

TECHNIQUE #7

Muster Willpower

NOT ALL QUITS ARE A BARREL OF LAUGHS. EVEN IF THEY ARE THE MOST REASONABLE IN THE WORLD, CERTAIN QUITS PRODUCE NOTHING BUT PAIN, CONFUSION, AND LONGING. THESE QUITS ARE HARD TO EXECUTE AND HARD TO MAINTAIN. IN THE FACE OF THIS SORT OF ADVERSITY, THE MUSTER WILLPOWER TECHNIQUE IS OFTEN THE BEST WAY TO GO, AND CAN BE USED TO GREAT EFFECT IN CONJUNCTION WITH THE BE REASONABLE TECHNIQUE. WILLPOWER ALLOWS YOU TO STAVE OFF THE IMPULSE TO EAT THE CHOCOLATE CAKE OR KISS THE EX-BOYFRIEND OR SMOKE THE CIGARETTE WHEN THAT IS ALL YOU WANT TO DO.

MUSTERING WILLPOWER IS MOST COMMONLY USED WHEN QUITTING FOR HEALTH, WHICH IS TO SAY QUITTING THINGS THAT ARE BAD FOR YOU. THESE THINGS MOST COMMONLY

INCLUDE SMOKING CIGARETTES, DRINKING ALCOHOL, EATING UNHEALTHY FOOD, AND DOING DRUGS. QUITS FOR HEALTH GET A LOT OF ATTENTION, BUT NO ONE EVER REALLY WANTS TO DO THEM. TO FORSAKE YOUR CRUTCH, YOUR EXCUSE, YOUR METHOD OF ESCAPE, YOUR DISTRACTION, OR YOUR PLEASURE IS ALWAYS A CONSUMMATE DRAG. SHOW ME AN EX-SMOKER AND I'LL SHOW YOU A PERSON WHO WISHES SHE NEVER STARTED, NOT SOMEONE WHO IS GLAD SHE QUIT. CALLING ON WILLPOWER MAKES THE QUIT FOR HEALTH POSSIBLE. NOTHING MAKES IT PLEASANT.

WILLPOWER SHOULD NOT BE CONFUSED WITH QUITTING; TO RESIST IS NOT THE SAME AS TO REJECT. MUSTER WILLPOWER IS A STRATEGY TO BE USED SPARINGLY, ONLY WHEN ABSOLUTELY NECESSARY. IF EVERY QUIT YOU EXECUTE INVOLVES LOTS OF WILLPOWER, YOU'RE PROBABLY QUITTING THE WRONG THINGS.

Retroactive Quitting: Myth or Reality?

Retroactive quitting a tricky concept, and occupies a tenuous position in the framework of the quitting way. Retroactive quitting refers to a quit that occurred in a quitter's past, without the quitter's knowledge, and is only identified as a quit on reflection.*

A quitter wakes up one day and realizes he has not flossed in six months. When the realization hits, the quitter feels glad and comments to himself that there is way too much flossing going on in the world anyway. When the quitter looks in the medicine cabinet for the floss to throw it away, it is already gone. Floss and flossing are things of the past. A quit has definitely taken place—the question is when. Did it occur half a year ago when the quitter last flossed, or that very morning when it crossed the quitter's mind?

When is a quit a quit—when the activity has stopped, or when the stopping of the activity has been identified and acknowledged?

A quitter wakes up one morning and realizes he has a full beard. He hasn't shaved his face in days, not as a result of a fully formed decision, but just because. Looking in the mirror,

* Retroactive quitting can best be compared with the concept of retroactive infidelity, which is betrayal in the form of a love affair that happened before an individual became involved with his current love interest. The love affair was not illicit at the time, because the current love interest wasn't on the scene, but transforms itself into infidelity retroactively as a result of jealous rages, obsessive rumination, and bad feelings on the part of the new love interest. He is, naturally, both completely justified and completely unjustified in these feelings.

he has many thoughts on the social implications of taking a razor to one's face every day, the environmental impact of shaving cream, the amount of time it takes to shave, and what his love interest will think of the beard. He resolves not to shave anymore, just trim a little here and there. A quit has taken place. Did it occur the first time this quitter failed to get out the razor, or did it occur when the notion to quit shaving came into his head, concrete and formed?

A quitter looks up into the starry, starry sky one evening and realizes he has stopped caring about the future of a failing love affair, and has not put any time or energy or even anxiety into it for a long time. A quit of the most private nature has crept up and asserted itself. The quitter, at this point, accepts and embraces this state of affairs—but when, exactly, did the quitter quit caring?

In the case of retroactive quitting, the question of volition comes into play. Can a quitter quit without realizing it? Does an action qualify as a quit if it is not an act of will? Can the very first step of any quit—thinking about it—be foregone? The central question is as follows: Is retroactive quitting a myth, nothing more than a fancy way of labeling the actions of literally thoughtless quitters, or is it a reality, the accurate description of a particular mode of quitting that has two very distinct stages: the quit and, later, the awareness of the quit?

Each quitter must decide how he will write his quitting history, and be very honest and not pull any fast ones. We all know how impolite revisionist history is. We all know how very easy it would be to make our own quitting careers seem more glamorous or thoughtful than they actually are by marshaling all kinds of semantic help, including the retroactive quit, to tidy the frayed edges.

However, every quitter finds it necessary, at some point in his quitting career, to call on the retroactive quit for autobiographical purposes. And well you should. Nasty accusations, usually leveled by antiquitters, of back pedaling, track covering, and history rewriting arise from a refusal to recognize the subterranean nature of certain quits.

The mythology of quitting says that the quitter is always sure, decisive, and fully in control when dealing the final blow. Not so. The quitter does not always know his own mind. The quitter is not always aware of what he is doing. This does not keep the quitter from quitting. If a tree falls in the middle of a forest, of course it makes a sound. Ignorance on the part of the quitter does not erase the occurrence of the quit.

TECHNIQUE #8

Be Passive-Aggressive

The Passive-Aggressive Quit is most often used by quitters extricating themselves from love affairs gone bad, but it is also effective in the working world. Engage in bad behavior, conduct yourself in an obnoxious or unseemly way, or be offensive or irritating all the time until you force what you are trying to quit to quit you.

You hate your job, but you need the unemployment benefits, so you get yourself fired. You can't take being the one to strike the final blow, and don't want to be accused of loving and leaving, so you act like a jerk until your girlfriend feels like a fool for sticking around for so long, can't take it anymore, and leaves you. One of you is a quitter. It's not her.

TECHNIQUE #9

Get Fed Up

Take on a long-suffering attitude toward whatever it is you are about to quit. Be frustrated by it on a regular basis. Be insulted and outraged that the thing exists at all. Talk about how lousy the whole situation is.

You've had it up to here. You're sick and tired. You've lived with it long enough. You can barely stand to think about it at all. When you have fully explored and expressed every ounce of frustration, quit. Feel completely justified. Get prickly if someone tries to play devil's advocate. If anyone points out that your attitude lacks perspicacity or is unfair, turn mean.

A brilliant display of the Get Fed Up technique can be found in the pages of recent theater history: Evan Handler, the star of I HATE HAMLET, executed a Get Fed Up of dramatic proportions during the play's run in 1991. Handler's costar, with whom he had had escalating difficulties, departed from the arranged choreography during a dueling scene and actually hit Handler with the flat part of his sword. This was the last straw. Handler walked off the stage in the middle of the performance and gave his notice on the way out of the theater.

Private Quitting

The private quit is a mysterious beast. Its ins and outs are slippery, its motivations complicated, and its execution a delicate undertaking. Naturally, the private quit goes under several different names, including the personal quit, the undercover quit, and the sly quit. If you can get the private quitter to talk about his quits, you have performed a minor miracle, and so there is little information on the actual anatomy of the private quit. The private quitter lives by the maxim that his ideas are nobody's business but his own. The same goes for his quits.

Private quitters are an interesting bunch, typically blessed with complex inner lives and the charisma of mystery. Why would a quitter be so concerned with executing a quit in utter privacy, in the dark of night, someplace under a rock where nobody can see? Hard to say. Private quitters have reasons of their own. Part of the drive to quit privately arises from an aversion to discussing motivations and rationales that are better left unspoken, impossible to describe, embarrassing, or nobody else's business. Perhaps the private quitter is so humble he does not want to take credit for the quit. Perhaps the private quitter is so vain he thinks no one else could possibly get it. Perhaps the private quitter is a purist, and wants his quit to remain uncorrupted by the opinions, thoughts, and advice of other people.

The private quitter spends a lot of time in the privacy of his own mind, which makes idea quitting a natural choice when it comes to type of quit. Quitting a belief in God and Country, changing philosophical stances, and quitting various personality traits are all material for the private quit. However, idea quits that thrive on recognition and attention from the outside world, like repudiation, secession from nations, and certain types of revolution, are not appropriate for the quitter interested in keeping things under wraps.

Although idea quits are common material for the private quitter, it is also possible to undertake quits belonging to the other

The Private Quit Is All the Quitter's Own

quitting fields—person, location, job, habit, and thing—privately. Logistically speaking, these types of quits will eventually be revealed, although the quitter himself may be long gone, literally or otherwise, and not available for comment. Even private quits come out in the wash.

The private quit is not for the insecure quitter. If a quitter needs a band of cheerleaders to clap their hands and stomp their feet over how brave, cool, or reckless the quit is, the private quit is a ridiculous choice. In fact, a hazard of private quitting is the solitude required to properly execute the quit. Because of the nature of their work, private quitters often become lonely and detached, entrenched in great, even glorified, isolation.

In this case, the hazards of loneliness, isolation, and detachment take on a hint of the sublime: Quitting is an essentially solitary activity, and for a quitter to immerse himself fully in the solitude of quitting via the private quit is to embrace not only the quitting process but the nature of quitting itself.

There is some debate as to whether the private quit can be accomplished by anyone other than an exclusively private quitter who has practiced and honed the skill, using the method throughout his quitting career. Many people feel this is a highly specialized area, novices and dilettantes beware. There is some truth to this, because the private quit necessitates a restraint not found in great quantities in most quitters—or, for that matter, most people. However, if the quitter finds himself literally speechless on the topic of the quit or physically sick at the idea of revealing its nuts and bolts, a private quit may well be in order.

Quitters embarking on a private quit must be prepared to cover their tracks on a regular basis. Simple questions like What did you do today? and How's tricks? are fertile ground for the giving out of all kinds of information, and can be disastrous for the private quitter. The private quitter must be committed to keeping his own secrets, and must always err on the side of caution when it comes to letting go of information. The private quitter is married to autonomy. The private quitter proposes to be an island. The private quitter never blows his cover.

TECHNIQUE #10

Quit in the Clutch

Quitting in the Clutch, or the eleventh-hour quit, has saved many a procrastinating quitter from becoming entrenched in inadvisable, irreparable embroilments. Quitting in the Clutch is sudden and often inexplicable. It is also often devastating, inconvenient, and shocking to everyone involved. The eleventh-hour quit precipitates immediate, large-scale consequences; this normally suits the quitter just fine, because she is operating in emergency quitting mode and is banking on the high and fast returns the eleventh-hour quit promises.

The great economy and flair of Quitting in the Clutch has made it something of the darling of the quitting world, rivaled only by Quitting While You Are Ahead, its diametric opposite. It has all kinds of dramatic possibilities, and is often depicted in movies and works of fiction.* Even so, eleventh-hour quitting should be used

*Ingrid Bergman not showing up at the train station in *Casablanca*, leaving Humphrey Bogart standing on the platform in the rain, is a classic cinematic treatment of the devastating effects of an eleventh-hour quit.

SPARINGLY. IT IS THE LAST OUT, THE ESCAPE HATCH, THE FINAL OPTION. IF A QUITTER FEEDS ON A STEADY DIET OF ELEVENTH-HOUR QUITTING, SHE RUNS THE RISK OF CORRUPTING THE FORM, DEPLETING IMPORTANT QUITTING ENERGY, AND LOOKING FOOLISH. TOO MUCH ELEVENTH-HOUR QUITTING IS LIKE CRYING WOLF. WATCH OUT. PEOPLE MIGHT STOP TAKING YOU SERIOUSLY.

ON THE OTHER HAND, IF THE QUITTER IS HIGHLY SELECTIVE AND PRECISE, AND ONLY EXECUTES A HANDFUL OF QUITS OVER THE COURSE OF AN ENTIRE CAREER, THE ELEVENTH-HOUR QUIT IS OFTEN THE MODE OF CHOICE. IT IS BIG, EFFECTIVE, UNMISTAKABLE, AND, ALMOST BY DEFINITION, INSPIRED. REFUSE TO WALK DOWN THE AISLE. DON'T GET ON THE PLANE. DON'T SIGN THE PAPERS. DRIVE PAST THE EXIT. WITHDRAW YOUR CANDIDACY JUST BEFORE THE VOTES ARE COUNTED. DON'T SHOW UP TO DEFEND YOUR DOCTORAL DISSERTATION. MISS YOUR CUE. THE SHOW WILL NOT NECESSARILY GO ON.

The Principled Quit

The principled quit must be embarked upon with a goal in mind. The quitter is always making a statement, never underestimates the P.R. value of a quit, and gets as much mileage out of it as possible. If done correctly, the principled quitter's quits often make the papers. The Duke of Windsor, who is the uncontested star of principled quitting, abdicated the throne of England, operating on the principle that if his country would not accept the woman with whom he was in love, he could not possibly be its king. "I now quit altogether public affairs and lay down my burden," he

said in an address that was broadcast around the world. Principled quitters love a sacrifice and are no strangers to martyrdom.

Because the principled quit often involves ethics, values, or morals, the principled quitter can be the most irritating among adherents to the quitting way. Vegetarians who make dying cow noises when they go out to dinner with people who order hamburgers, environmentalists who have quit using aerosol spray cans and lecture people who still do, and ex-smokers who can't be in a room that has ever contained an ashtray are cases in point.

The principled quit is often used as a strategy for changing the world, and quitters band together for this purpose. Boycotts, strikes, and secession from unions are common group quits executed for the sake of a principle.

Principled quitters should not be confused with faddish quitters who jump, without a principle in sight, on whatever quitting bandwagon is rolling past. Quitting wearing bell-bottom jeans because they went out of fashion is not the same as quitting wearing a bra as a form of social activism. Quitting eating butter because everyone has replaced it with margarine is not the same as quitting eating green grapes in support of the grape-pickers' strike.

If the cause is popular, faddish quitters often join the ranks of principled quitters working toward a goal. The principled quitters are generally glad to have them, because there is strength in numbers.

Unfortunately, faddish quitters cannot be counted on to quit and keep on quitting until the goal is accomplished. This is not because they are independent agents likely to up and quit with agendas of their own, but because another quitting trend is always on the horizon, and the faddish quitter tends to privilege what is current.

The principled quit can be accomplished using a number of techniques. The Muster Willpower is often used ingeniously by principled quitters: Gandhi didn't starve to death, but he held off eating and made a point. Making a Scene is also a good strategy for the principled quitter—witness the sit-down strike—and the Be Reasonable is a favorite, because the principled quitter is always positive he is doing the right thing and likes summoning evidence to prove it. Martin Luther came up with 95 theses to back up quitting major tenets of the Catholic church, which he did entirely on principle, and posted them accordingly.

TECHNIQUE #11

Repudiate Your Ideas

Disown opinions for which you once would have gone to the wall. Meticulously enumerate every little way in which you were mistaken. Apologize for your previous wrong-headedness. Reject the truth as you once conceived of it, even if you have converted other people or written manifestos on the subject and signed them with your own blood. If you have always insisted that marriage is a meaningless institution, have a huge fancy wedding in a church; in your vows, expound on the virtues of matrimony. Like Ludwig Wittgenstein, write a whole book completely contradicting your original philosophy; like Bertrand Russell, run around to lecture halls telling people you have changed your mind.

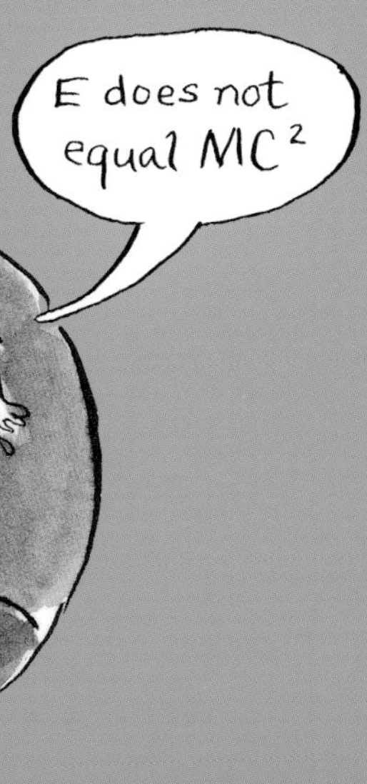

Quitting Before Beginning and Quitting While You Are Ahead

Because quitting is so much work, some quitters choose to simplify and streamline the process by quitting before they begin. The quitter quits before the thing to be quit wedges itself in, before it takes hold and starts to matter. By rejecting the thing to be quit right off the bat, ambivalence is avoided. The whole pro-and-con quitting game, where the quitter isn't sure, kind of likes the thing he is quitting, and wants to weigh things before he jumps to the quit, is made irrelevant. Furthermore, the quitter does not waste a lot of time evaluating or despairing over the thing about to be quit. The quitter has already checked out and has no stake whatsoever in the person, place, or thing he is quitting. Quitting before beginning involves high levels of detachment and is marked by a total and unregenerate lack of engagement.

Go into a love affair absolutely sure it will never last. Do not, at any point, try to rescue it from demise. Move to a place knowing full well you cannot possibly stay. Don't have your mail forwarded, make any friends, or bring clothes warm enough for the upcoming season. When in a restaurant, order food you know you will not like. Pick at it. Don't eat a bite.

The idea of quitting before beginning tends to beg the following question: Why bother? Why bother doing a thing if you have already quit it? It is inconsiderate and rude to second-guess other people's quits. And anyway, the far better question is Why bother doing anything at all? Nothing lasts forever. Every activity is a quit waiting to happen. If a quitter wants to cut to the chase and save a little time, why shouldn't he? After all, the quitter has better things to do than sit around and wait to quit.

Part of the beauty and appeal of quitting is that the quitter takes control and imposes will on circumstance. Quitters are in the unique position of being able to kidnap the inevitable (all things come to an end) by beating it to the punch.

Although quitting before beginning is the high road to avoiding involvement that will only end in a quit, it requires great presence of mind and is extremely demanding. The economy of this tactic may be attractive to many quitters but it is suited only to some. Quitting before beginning requires great clarity: The quitter must be able to identify what he does not want.

If things have advanced to a stage where the time for quitting before beginning is past, the next best option is to quit while you are ahead. Recognize a good thing. Be satisfied and preserve it. Cut decay off at the pass. Like quitting before beginning, quitting while you are ahead is a time-saving device as well as a way of averting the pain and misery of activities and involvements that are doomed to failure.

It is often difficult to tell when you are ahead, and so the quitter must employ a sort of foresight akin to clairvoyance. This includes recognizing impending doom, approaching ruin, advancing decay or dissolution, desperate optimism, and one's own denial of the rule that all good things are temporary.

The quitter's special foresight can be traced to a healthy quitting instinct. The healthy quitting instinct is a desire to nip failure in the bud coupled with a good sense of timing. If the quitter is not sufficiently afraid of failure, the quitter should look closely at the failure of others. If the quitter is not blessed with a native sense of timing, he should cultivate one by noting the poorly timed quits of others. Do not let your good quitting instinct be derailed by distraction or torpor or drowsiness. Do not fail to quit while you are ahead simply because you are not paying attention. Don't sit around in a fog or a stupor or a slump and watch things go down the tubes.

Hall of fame quitters who quit while they were ahead include Margaret Mitchell, who quit writing after completing *Gone With the Wind*, The Beatles, who broke up before they fell apart, and Jim Brown, star running back for the National Football League's Cleveland Browns, who quit football four games after his most brilliant run. His words, "I quit with regret but no sorrow," should serve as inspiration and comfort for quitters the world around.

TECHNIQUE #12

Abandon and Conceal

THE ABANDON AND CONCEAL IS THE QUITTER'S VERY OWN. IT BOLSTERS QUITTING CONFIDENCE AND GIVES THE QUITTER A SENSE OF GREAT PERSONAL IMPORTANCE. ALSO KNOWN AS THE SECRET QUIT, ABANDON AND CONCEAL IS A SECRET WEAPON BECAUSE IT GOES UTTERLY UNDETECTED BY THE OUTSIDE WORLD. YOU LEAVE NO CLUES, SO NO ONE WILL DISCOVER, CHALLENGE, OR CORRUPT WHAT YOU HAVE DONE. QUIT TAKING YOUR VITAMINS. QUIT WEARING UNDERWEAR. QUIT READING FOOTNOTES. QUIT BELIEVING IN GERMS.

TECHNIQUE #13

Take Revenge

The Take Revenge method is often used in conjunction with Make a Scene. In this case, the vengeful quitter knows no bounds of decency, is not concerned for her soul, and goes for the jugular.

Step one: Hold a grudge and harbor hatred. Step two: Carefully design a quit that will cause trouble, satisfy your penchant for sabotage, and give rein to the full scope of your vindictiveness. Step three: Seek and find retribution through your quit.

Your best friend steals your boyfriend. Act like you're really glad the two of them are so happy. Pretend you are unselfish and able to rise above it. At the wedding, when the minister asks anyone who knows a reason why these two should not be lawfully joined to speak now or forever hold their peace, stand up and say the groom is

the biggest jerk on the face of the earth, the bride is a bottom feeder, you know for a fact that they are involved in a transcontinental drug ring, and you are hereby making a citizen's arrest. Ruin the wedding.

If you are not a dramatic quitter given to high-visibility maneuvers, Take Revenge can be used as a companion to other techniques, such as Be Passive-Aggressive or Abandon and Conceal. In this case, the quitter seeks to undermine the person on whom she is taking revenge and render her powerless, ridiculous, or insignificant.

In grade school, your teacher made you write your cursive capital letters over and over until you did them properly and they looked just like his. When you grow up, you quit writing in cursive altogether, quietly avenging yourself on your grade school teacher by flooding the world with printing.

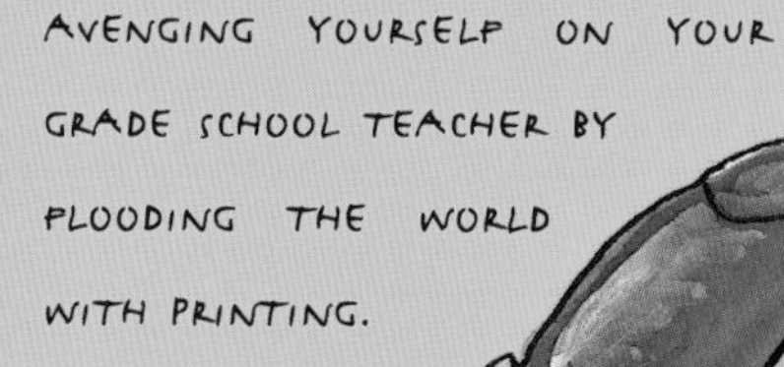

The Requit

One of the essential tenets of the quitting way is Always Move On. Backward time travel is a difficult thing for anyone, and generally a closed option for the quitter. There is, however, one method of quitting that allows for temporary time travel for the purposes of reaffirming an already accomplished quit. It is known as the requit.

Generally, the requit works like this: The quitter returns to the scene of the quit, approximates prequit circumstances, and executes the quit all over again.

Call your ex-boyfriend on the telephone. Say things like "You were in my dream last night," "I think you'd really like this book I'm reading," "The guy who just moved in next door reminds me a lot of you," or "I thought I saw you at the supermarket the

other day." Decide you must see him. Say so. If you live far away, get on a plane as soon as possible. If you live close by, hang up and go over to his house immediately. Install yourself there and act like you are his girlfriend. Cook dinner, go to the movies, use his toothbrush. After a very short time, realize that all his habits are irritating, that he does not understand you, that he is not the love of your life, and that you cannot possibly spend another minute with him. Start acting weird. Instigate a bitter fight, heated discussion, or tearful silence during which you tell him the whole thing is impossible. Say everything you said the last time you broke up, and then leave.

Like the renewal of wedding vows, the requit reaffirms and solidifies the original quit. Repetition is a great learning tool, and the quitter's revisitation of the quit serves to clarify the quit and expunge any lingering doubts about its value and durability. Requitting is a way for the quitter to make sure, to tighten the lug bolts, to dig her heels into the quit. In addition, the requit often provides a little drama, jump-starting the quitting euphoria upon which most quitters thrive.

The requit is best staged in a state of semiawareness and confusion. A reasonable frame of mind is not fertile ground for a requit. For one thing, reasonableness will make it difficult for the quitter to suspend disbelief in the plausibility of the time travel.

Also, the quitter must work herself into a fever pitch in order to carry herself through the requit, which depends on momentum. The quitter performing the requit must never stop to question herself, and must avoid being questioned by others at all costs. Any kind of static will slow the quitter down, disarm the quitter, and prevent the requit from being fully executed.

The requit is best suited—perhaps, in fact, only suited—to person quitting. The degree of desperation and frenzy required to pull off a requit can rarely be drummed up without another human being providing emotional fodder for the quitter to work with (or, more precisely, against). Occasionally, other quitting fields will suffice, but there is nothing like a warm body to inspire a requit and snap a quitter into high gear.

With the requit, you're in and you're out. No messing around with details, exploring your true emotions, or considering anyone's feelings. You don't have to know what you're doing. You just have to do it. The requit is commonly achieved in the heat of a frenetic quitting passion. Like the eleventh-hour quit, a spiritual twin of the requit, the requit cannot be thought through in advance or discussed with a second party, particularly the party the quitter is requitting.

The quitter should only attempt a requit with an utter lack of care and foresight. This will obscure—and even eclipse—the risks imbedded in the requit. Every requit is a potential disaster. If embarked upon without the necessary momentum, it becomes quicksand. The risk is multiplied by the fact that the quitter personality is not naturally disposed to going backward in time; it is the quitting way to rely on the idea that time marches on, even through the most inclement weather. The requit can easily backfire, drawing the quitter back in to the prequit state instead of accomplishing its goal—to revitalize the quit and extricate the quitter once and for all.

TECHNIQUE #14

Burn a Bridge

Spit in the face of responsible decision making. Refuse to keep your options open. Alienate yourself completely from those you love, work for, or trust. With this method in hand, you will be fearless. Consequences of the quit will be rendered powerless to daunt because burning bridges means you don't care. Previous quits will pale in comparison.

Quit the job you have had for most of your adult life. In your exit interview, tell your boss he has bad taste in suits and couldn't manage the contents of a grocery bag. Say that you are embarrassed to have ever worked for him and that his toaster could make better decisions. Tell him you wouldn't name him as a reference if you were starving.

Although Bridge Burners tend to be aggressive people, some are less dramatic than others. The Bridge Burns they undertake tend to be subversive, silent, and tortured in nature. The subversive Bridge Burn usually stays concealed

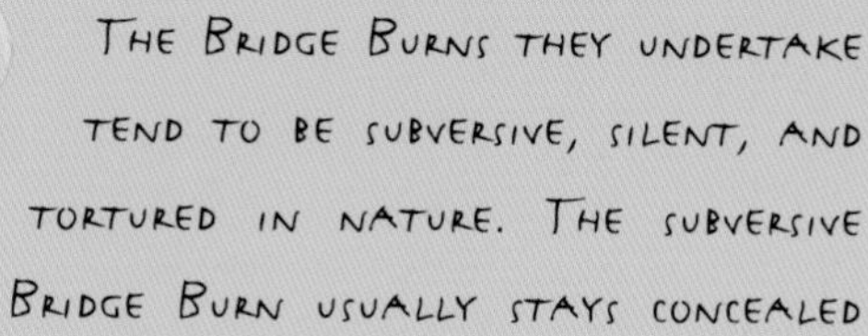

until only ashes remain. It is the pyromania of the angry, offended, or disgusted quitter, and often used as a weapon for retribution. The subversive Bridge Burn, especially when employed in conjunction with Take Revenge, is a favorite tactic of the irate private quitter, and is often used as a form of punishment. Subversive Bridge Burning means you don't think the person on the bridge deserves to know that it has gone up in flames.

A friend with whom you are very close, who knows all your secrets and fears and hopes, somehow betrays, irrevocably disappoints, or terribly offends you. Say nothing. If he or she asks what's wrong, lie. Say everything is fine. Suddenly become totally unavailable. Don't call or write or visit. If the friend manages to contact you, be cold. If possible, manipulate mutual friends into reporting that you are doing just great—but only attempt this if you are sure you can do it without tipping your hand and revealing that you actually care what the burned party thinks about you.

Give no clues, hope you are doing maximum psychological damage, and never speak to the friend again.

TECHNIQUE #15

Sulk

WHEN PEOPLE ASK YOU WHY YOU WALKED OFF THE COURT IN THE MIDDLE OF THE GAME OR WHY YOU REFUSED TO WRITE THE REST OF THE BOOK OR WHY YOU DROPPED OUT OF THE SENATE RACE, TELL THEM YOU DID IT BECAUSE YOU FELT LIKE IT. BE COMPLETELY NONCOMMUNICATIVE. IGNORE FURTHER QUESTIONS. IF THEY PERSIST, SHRUG YOUR SHOULDERS AND SLUMP IN YOUR CHAIR. POUT. GIVE THEM THE EYE ROLL. SAY IT DOESN'T MATTER ANYWAY. SAY YOU DON'T CARE.

The Unquit and Quitting the Quit: A Discussion

Vulnerable quitters racked by doubt and confusion often find themselves wanting to undo what they have done. The quitter hates his postquit life, wishes he had never monkeyed around with things in the first place, is sure that unhappiness is better than uncertainty, and longs, in general, for the security of the past, regardless of how miserable it may have been. Furthermore, quitters daunted by postquitting emptiness and confusion often take it upon themselves to revise history. The dark, gloomy, unsatisfying cave of a life that the quitter quit becomes, in the quitter's flawed memory, a well-set-up middle-class home in the suburbs with award-winning rose bushes and apple pies cooling on the windowsill.

Faced with this depression and delusion, the quitter often considers the possibility of executing what is sometimes erroneously referred to as an unquit—to unravel the quit and fully reinstate prequit circumstances, to return to the status quo that existed before the quit.

This process, however, is entirely impossible. Once the status quo is interrupted, it is gone forever. Once you quit, nothing is ever the same again. The euphoria is addictive; you develop an appetite for volition; you lose a certain innocence. You change. Consequently, your relationship to the thing that you quit shifts.

In addition, the thing you quit may well have changed, either as a result of your absence or the natural progression of time. Your girlfriend has changed her hairdo, her habits, and her attitude; your university is full of people that you don't know who espouse strange ideas; your city's subway system has suffered a fare increase and your old neighborhood has been gentrified. Things in the world outside of you shift just as surely as your attitude toward them alters. You can never go back to holding hands, and you can't unquit a quit. The desire to return fully to prequit circumstances can never be fulfilled.

On the other hand, if a quitter is fully aware that the progress of time is a real thing with real implications and is still in the market to welcome the thing quit back into his life, there is a way to proceed. Every quit is a decision, but not every quit is a final decision. It is the nature and prerogative of the quitter to change his mind. When a quitter returns to a thing quit, it is naturally by way of quitting again. This procedure is known as quitting the quit.

For example, a quitter may quit smoking. Soon thereafter, the quitter may realize the quit was ill-advised. At this point, the quitter may decide to quit quitting smoking, and thus the quitter smokes again. Presto.

Nonquitters often misname quitting the quit, terming it "recidivism," "backsliding," or "falling off the wagon." This is unfortunate, and is yet another example of the liberties many nonquitters take with the language.

If the quitter encounters guilt, self-loathing, or static from nonquitters after quitting the quit, he should remember the following attributes of the quitter personality:

Quitters cut their losses.

Quitters admit their mistakes.

Quitters change their minds.

These qualities are part of the quitter soul and allow the quitter substantial latitude. If you can cut your losses, you can afford to suffer many of them; if you can admit your mistakes, you can afford to make a lot of them; if you can change your mind, you can change it as often as you please. It is the lot of the quitter to constantly reevaluate which activities ought to stay and which ought to be quit. Embrace your lot. Reevaluate and act. Quit the quit.

TECHNIQUE #16

Plot and Endure

SCHEME ABOUT WHEN AND HOW YOU WILL EXECUTE YOUR QUIT. SPEND ALL YOUR SPARE TIME LOOKING FORWARD TO IT, AND CONVINCE YOURSELF THAT YOU CAN TOLERATE ANYTHING AS LONG AS YOU KNOW THERE'S AN END IN SIGHT. FOCUS ON THE LIGHT AT THE END OF THE TUNNEL. REVEL IN YOUR SUFFERING, KNOWING THAT YOU WILL SOMEDAY BE RELEASED. LIE IN WAIT FOR THE PERFECT MOMENT, THEN EXECUTE THE QUIT.

On the Lingering Quit

The lingering quit is characterized by excessive rumination and the chewing up of a lot of time. The quitter prepares for the quit weeks or months in advance, often making minor quitting noises and usually obsessing on the quit that looms ahead. After the quitter finally quits, she draws things out so that although the quit has technically been executed, nothing really changes, and life, for a long time, is all about the pervasive, endless, lingering quit.

During this period, the quitter waits for logistical details to work themselves out, creates more of them as needed, obsesses, worries, and generally monkeys with the quit, teasing and prodding until there is nothing left and the quitter is forced to move on.

Classic examples of the lingering quit include:

1. Continuing to live with your boyfriend for months on end after quitting him. Sometimes includes sharing a bed and trying to remember why you have decided to break things off. You are free, but you are not really free.

2. Giving lots and lots of notice when you quit your job. Usually includes tying up loose ends that do not exist and encouraging your coworkers to quit. You are a lame duck. You are there, but you are not really there.

3. Taking a really long time to pack and say good-bye when you quit your city. Includes endlessly sorting through all your possessions, thinking about the past, and making every encounter, for months on end, a drawn-out good-bye scene.

The lingering quit is diametrically opposed to the clean break, which, though something of a chimera, is still pursued by many a hopeful quitter. The clean break is marked by total and immediate closure, with no remorse and no regret. No quitter needs to make apologies for running around after the clean break like some kind of fountain of youth if that's what she wants to do, but that doesn't give anyone a license to talk trash about the lingering quit. All methods of quitting have their advantages. When you execute a lingering quit, you get to know it like the back of your hand. You can map its progress in your sleep. A hardcore, close-knit relationship is forged between you and your quit, as intimate as it is miserable. The lingering quit is a testament to drawn-out endings, painful delays, and all manner of emotional loitering. The lingering quit is a true test of the quitter's mettle.

The lingering quit is not for quitters with short attention spans, somewhere to be in a hurry, or anything major to distract them from the quit. If the lingering quit feels interminable, the quitter knows she is doing it right. If the quitter is spending less than 75 percent of her time thinking about the quit, the quitter is either not proceeding properly or is not executing a lingering quit. What looks like a lingering quit may be some other quitting technique (the Plot and Endure, for example, is often mistaken for a lingering quit), which may be just as satisfying but not nearly as relentless or perverse.

The lingering quit is perfect for the dog days of summer, particularly if the quitter lives in an especially humid part of the country

or a large city where people are piled up on top of one another and summer seems to stretch on and on. A summer lingering quit will exacerbate the quitter's feeling of endless, swampy embroilment by making the quit seem to take even longer than it does. The summer lingering quit is especially intolerable, and is therefore recommended to heighten the quitter's quitting experience.

TECHNIQUE #17

Deny Involvement

THIS TRICK OF THE TRADE ALLOWS THE QUITTER TOTAL FREEDOM. IN THE FACE OF DENIAL, THE REALITY OF YOUR SITUATION IS TOTALLY IMMATERIAL. TO EMPLOY DENY INVOLVEMENT PROPERLY, YOU WILL BE FORCED TO IGNORE THE TRUTH AND TO LIE OUTRIGHT. DENY EVER HAVING SIGNED THE LEASE TO YOUR APARTMENT, MUCH LESS CROSSED THE THRESHOLD. CLAIM YOU HAVE NEVER HEARD OF THE COMPANY YOU WORK FOR. SAY THAT YOU NEVER EVEN APPLIED TO THE COLLEGE YOU ARE DROPPING OUT OF. INSIST THAT YOU'VE NEVER MET THE PERSON YOU ARE MARRIED TO.

KEEP IN MIND THAT THE USE OF THIS TECHNIQUE WILL INSPIRE INTENSE ANIMOSITY AND SUSPICION IN OTHER PEOPLE. OTHER HIGH-IMPACT, POTENTIALLY HOSTILE QUITTING TECHNIQUES LIKE THE BRIDGE BURN OR MAKE A SCENE ARE CHILD'S PLAY COMPARED WITH DENY INVOLVEMENT.

On Quitting an Obsession

Obsession is a high-maintenance thing, requiring a relentless spirit to keep it alive. Obsession is, in fact, a monument to perseverance, and perseverance is no friend to the quitting way.

Happily, while all obsessors are driven and fueled by the same crazy, inexplicable energy, many obsessors are also very fickle. The fickle obsessor jumps from one minor obsession to the next at the drop of a hat. Though each obsession is, for a short period, all-consuming, in the end, one obsession is as good as another for the fickle obsessor. Despite the inherent contradictions between the quitting way and the world of obsession, fickle obsessors often make great quitters. For the fickle obsessor, the key to quitting an obsession is to enter into an obsession with the quit. While quitting, he can think only of how, why, and when the quit will occur. The quit sponges up all the effort the obsessor would normally spend on his obsession. Quitting a fixation on astrology, for example, would be accomplished by obsessively going through your address book and using white-out to erase the sun signs of all the people in it, which you once obsessively found out and marked down; carefully avoiding the horoscope page of the magazines you read; and throwing away every book you bought on the subject.

Then there are those obsessors who are completely steadfast, and would never trade their obsession for any other, including an obsession with a quit. These types have a long row to hoe. Lifelong fixations sap unbelievable amounts of time and energy: It is all the person can do to woo only one love interest, write the great American novel, or find the fountain of youth, the holy grail, or the cure for a terrible disease. Not surprisingly, lifelong, one-object obsessors have little to show in the way of quitting. They have no desire to quit the obsession and no time to quit things unrelated to it. What's to quit? these types may ask. There is no answer except to wish them the best of luck, kiss them good-bye, and hope to see them in quitting heaven, where it seems that obsessive people must also go, as there is a mysterious affinity between the two camps, each of which cull members from the same soup of strugglers.

For those who are not hopeless lifelong obsessors (and thus useless at quitting) or fickle obsessors (who employ their own special quitting method—obsessing on the quit), but just regular quitters caught in the maelstrom of an obsession, the following methods are often useful for extrication:

1. *Go cold turkey.* Often cited as the most effective method for quitting obsessions. This is the all-at-once, rev-up-briefly-and-then-do-it-with-startling-resolution way. This method

is usually not realistic when the object of the obsession is a person, but works well otherwise. Your obsession with the *New York Times* crossword puzzle is out of hand. Do not just quit trying to do the Sunday puzzle, quit trying to do any puzzles, and quit buying the *New York Times* altogether. Your obsession with the Lucky Seven scratch-and-win lottery has reached mammoth proportions. Pick a day, and on that day quit buying the scratch-and-win cards forever more. Never take another chance again.

2. *Practice contingency quitting.* Contingency quitting is expressed in terms of if/then statements. "If my obsession with reading *The Phenomenology of Spirit* cover to cover starts to make me weak in the head, then I will quit." "If my obsessive picking of nonexistent blemishes on my face begins to make me look like a chickenpox patient, then I will quit picking." "If my obsessive concern with the weather forecast makes me actually prepare for the weather the weatherman predicts, then I will quit listening to it." If the obsession is worth quitting, the contingency will soon come to pass. Your tendency to quit will overrule your tendency to obsess.

3. *Demystify the obsession.* Become extremely analytical, laying the anatomy of your obsession bare. Take away the magic by revealing the nuts and bolts. Pick apart your obsession with

the U.S. Postal Service by considering at great length just why the possibility of receiving surprise letters and packages is so attractive to you. Ask yourself what it is deep within you that craves the possibility of your entire life changing with the opening of the mailbox, and what exactly the big deal is about breaking the seal of an envelope. This soul-searching process will make your obsession much less attractive, and will thus make it prime for quitting.

4. *Begin to harbor disgust for the object of your obsession.* Allow yourself to realize that the girl on whom you have a seemingly intractable fixation has big ears, an annoying way of sneezing, or a stupid message on her answering machine. Get the heebie jeebies about it. Be unable to shake the feeling of repulsion that has wedged its way into your mind. Allow the disgust

to branch out, infiltrate, and completely taint your feelings for the object of your obsession until it eclipses the obsession entirely. Proceed with the quit as you would under normal circumstances.

TECHNIQUE #18

Give Up

Throwing in the towel is a mainstay of the quitting way, and a must for anyone interested in a well-rounded quitting career. The only drawback of this technique is that it rarely provides much in the way of catharsis. Giving Up is gentle, often going unnoticed by anyone not intimately connected to the quitter. The actual moment of giving up is hard to place. The red carpet does not come unfurled; there's no big fireworks display; nobody cares.

Some quitters attempt to mitigate this feature of the Give Up technique by making a big show of it, but these attempts generally end in exhaustion, with little in the way of recognition. The headliner quitting techniques—Burning Bridges, Quitting in the Clutch, and the like—will always eclipse Giving Up when push comes to shove. It is best to let it be, and grant Giving Up its unsung place in the world of quitting.

ADMIT THAT YOU WILL NEVER MANAGE TO PAY YOUR BILLS ON TIME. LET THEM PILE UP. REALIZE THAT YOUR MOTHER WILL NEVER LAY OFF CALLING YOU AT SEVEN IN THE MORNING. GIVE UP TRYING TO GET HER TO STOP DIALING. UNDERSTAND THAT YOUR DENTIST DOES NOT REMEMBER YOUR NAME. GIVE UP REMINDING HIM. GIVE UP TRYING TO EXPLAIN THINGS TO PEOPLE WHO HAVE THEIR FINGERS IN YOUR MOUTH.

Quitting the Search for Happiness

Quitting the pursuit of happiness is one of the more cerebral quits, and as such can be something of a turn-off for the quitter accustomed to experience, action and adventure and running around a lot. Still, even dynamic quitters find themselves drawn to this difficult but worthy quit. Quitting the search for happiness (love, romance, fame, fortune, the contented or glamorous life) essentially means quitting the belief that things will get better. It relies on the tricky process of living in your allotted time zone with the hand you have been dealt. To do this, the quitter must stop putting stock in the future. Things are not sure to improve. Time does not heal all wounds. You may not experience an upswing. The pursuit of happiness arises from a stubborn fixation on the future. The future has no charm without hope and optimism, which give it shape. And so, hope and optimism are the true culprits here, always whispering in the wayward quitter's ear, saying hang on, happiness will come.

When quitting the pursuit of happiness, the quitter must first identify the role of hope and optimism in his life. What, exactly, is the quitter hoping for? What does the quitter wish for when he blows out his birthday candles? What does the quitter discuss with God during his nightly prayers? The quitter should try to be specific. Attempting to quit hope and optimism indiscriminately saps quitting energy and can lead to depression. Once the quitter has determined which sort of hope and optimism is at the root of the problem, the quitter should take steps to break hope and optimism down by not expressing them or allowing them to manifest themselves.

Following are some suggestions:

1. *Start small.* Quit putting on lipstick to go to the laundromat in hopes that the guy at the next machine will be cute. Quit reading the want ads in hopes that you will find a better job. Quit making small talk at parties in hopes that you will have an actual conversation and make a friend. Execute small quits to limber yourself up for the bigger and better work of giving up on happiness altogether.

2. *Stop waiting.* Waiting is contrary to the quitting way, because it is a clear indication that the quitter is harboring hope and optimism for one thing or another, and not picking to quit. The most pernicious form of waiting, in terms

of searching for happiness, is waiting for some undefined salvation—deliverance in the form of a person, an event, or an opportunity. This way of life can lead only to mishaps and cases of mistaken identity. Be assured that whatever you are waiting for will not be the answer.

3. *Stop believing in the power of positive thought.* Laugh scornfully at studies that allege to show that positive thinking, imaging, visualization, or prayer "work." Become convinced that any one potential future is as likely to come to pass as the next, regardless of what goes on between your two ears. Come to the conclusion that self-fulfilling prophecies—of both the positive and negative sort—are a fiction. Decide everything is random and beyond your control. Realize that the only way to exercise power over the search for happiness is to quit it.

4. *Quit accepting happiness as a desirable goal.* Notice it makes people seem lobotomized. Notice it is completely temporary. Notice it is not the only emotion in the world. Once you've rejected the idea of happiness, quitting the search for it is a foregone conclusion.

It should be noted, finally, that quitting the search for happiness is not the same as accepting misery. Accepting misery implies an unwillingness to tamper with the status quo.* In contrast, quitting the search for happiness is a rupture, a willful departure from fixation on the future, a throwing-off of the shackles of hope, optimism, and positive thinking. The quitter is left not with unhappiness but with a blank slate. The blank slate is a breeding ground for action. No longer hemmed in by strictly happiness-seeking activities, the quitter is free to investigate activity of all stripes. Go to the party even though you know it will be a drag. Read the newspaper even though you know it will depress you. Join a bowling league even though you know it's not the answer. Ante up at the poker table even though you know you will be dealt a lousy hand. Get out of bed even though you know you have nothing to look forward to. This rash of new activities is sure, at the very least, to produce a rash of new quitting possibilities.

* If you are in fact miserable and would prefer not to be, engage in process-of-elimination quitting. Single out and quit all the activities that actually make you miserable. Be methodical. Expunge them one by one. If there is a germ of happiness to be found, it will surface when you have quit everything obscuring it. (Process-of-elimination quitting is like process-of-elimination courting. Any and all qualities you consider ideal mean nothing in the final analysis; you can't possibly know what the love of your life is like until you meet her. Instead of searching for someone, process-of-elimination courting dictates that you reject people, one after the next, as they prove themselves unlovable, undesirable, or unsuitable. Continue until you are left with a person who does not inspire rejection. She is the one.)

TECHNIQUE #19

Take to Your Bed

The Take to Your Bed technique is helpful for the quitter at the end of her rope. It is suitable for use in quitting ideas (such as the notion that anything matters), hope for the future, and optimism of any kind. When despair is the operative emotion attending the quit, Take to Your Bed is the appropriate technique.

Collapse in a heap of depression and disillusionment, driven to your bed in a sweep of psychic exhaustion. Realize everything is hopeless. Intend never to emerge.

Although opting out is a staple of the quitting way, this particular incarnation of the notion requires a somewhat sedentary nature on the part of the quitter. Athletic quitters should take to their beds with caution.

Many quitters who take to their beds bring things with them, like magazines or cookies. Marcel Proust is a good example. He took paper and pen and wrote REMEMBRANCE OF THINGS PAST.

The Painful Quit and the Ill-Fated Quit: A Comparative Study

Although the painful quit and the ill-fated quit share many elements, there are several important differences.

First, some words on the painful quit:

The painful quit is not a joke. The painful quit can be devastating, and often takes weeks or months to take shape and reveal its true form. The painful quit often seems unreal, its cause and anatomy ephemeral and wraithlike. Often the quitter will forget why she is quitting, and must rely on quitter instinct alone to carry the quit to its completion.

When you quit a love interest for whom you have respect and admiration not because you think you will ever love someone else more but because you know you do not love this love interest enough, it is a painful quit. When you quit pursuing your aspiration not because you no longer want to be a rock star or an astronaut or a movie actress but because you know you are not good enough, it is a painful quit.

The painful quit appears in the quitter's dreams and at the bottom of the quitter's coffee cup. The quitter has trouble making simple decisions unrelated to the quit (what to cook for dinner, which socks to wear, and what to write in the "person to be contacted in case of emergency" line on forms), is reduced to tears

for no reason, and feels a sudden, inexplicable affinity for whatever is being quit.

Second, some words on the ill-fated quit:

Not everything always works out. Not everything is for the best. The quitter quits her sweetheart and never loves again. The quitter quits celebrating major holidays, and from that point on she feels a gaping hole in her spirituality.

It isn't just the outcome that marks the ill-fated quit. Much more, the actual process of the ill-fated quit feels off somehow, and produces anxiety even as the quitter is in the act of executing the quit. During the course of an ill-fated quit, the quitter may have visions related to the quit, feel a sense of doom, or know in her bones that the quit is a bad idea. The quitter is right: The quit is a bad idea. It is a horrible mistake and will probably haunt the quitter for the rest of her days. This is the nature of the ill-fated quit; it cannot be avoided. You will never get over it.

The ill-fated quit is something of a rite of passage for all quitters. If a quitter can continue to quit after an ill-fated quit, she has passed a milestone. Ill-fated quits have turned perfectly good quitters with promising quitting careers ahead of them into jaded, relentless detractors of the quitting way. On the other hand, many an ill-fated quit has served to strengthen the quitter's commitment to the quitting way. The quitter realizes that her whole life has taken shape partly as a result of the ill-fated quit, and even if the turn was essentially for the worse, the quitter revels in the fact that at least the decision was her own.

The essential similarity between painful and ill-fated quits is that they hold in common the same major occupational hazards: remorse and regret. The difference is whereas the remorse or regret connected to a painful quit will fade with time, the remorse or regret connected to an ill-fated quit will never go away, and can only be respected and admired.

Whereas remorse can be combated with a steam-roller attitude, flat-out denial, or new diversions, regret is a more insidious emotion. Regret can surface at any time, demanding attention, nourishment, and time. There is no real way to avoid regret if it is in the quitting atmosphere. You cannot disguise it, you cannot ignore it, and you cannot plan around it.

There are some salves to help alleviate the sear of both the painful quit and the ill-fated quit. Be advised that although nothing can cure regret, remorse and other subemotions of painful and ill-fated quits can be tackled, and sometimes quelled, in the following ways:

1. *Pretend it's all for the best.* The Pollyanna attitude works temporarily for some quitters. It can help to distract the quitter and ease the passage of time. Use the time you would normally spend with the only person you ever really loved—and have just quit—to balance your checkbook or organize your silverware drawer. Tell yourself how wonderful it is that you finally have time to do so.

2. *Pretend it wasn't your fault.* Displacing blame is often an effective balm for the quitter in pain. If you realize that you have quit the only job that ever challenged you, which you loved and worked toward for years, revise history and convince yourself that you were fired. Harbor hatred for your ex-boss and lay the blame at her feet with stunning disregard for the reality of the situation.

3. *Pretend it never happened at all.* Utter denial usually reduces pain to a minimum, although some may creep in at the edges when the quitter's defenses are down. Look at people like they are nuts when they ask you questions related to the quit. Do

not answer the questions. Claim to have no idea what they're talking about. Say you are just fine.

TECHNIQUE #20

Wipe the Slate Clean

Commonly known as the polyquit, Wiping the Slate Clean involves total departure from the status quo. The quitter starts and does not stop until there is nothing left to quit. An entire way of life is razed to the ground. Quit your love interest. Then quit your job. Then quit your city. Then quit your name and go by an alias. Start a whole new life.

Consider the Quit

The quit is an act of will. As an act of will, it is a form of expression. As a form of expression, it is an art. As an art, it can employ any raw material. The quit is not picky. You can quit fighting a war of attrition just as well as you can give up on a losing battle, just as well as you can desert in the middle of a victory.

Consider the quit at every juncture. You may be inspired to jump even if the ship isn't actually sinking. Always get out while you still can, but consider getting out the minute it crosses your mind.

Quit to combat stasis. Quit to avoid exhaustion. Quit as a method of crisis intervention. Quit to prove a point. Quit to see what you're made of. Quit because you are driven to it. Quit because you are inspired. Quit because you can.

"The trumpet is my enemy."

—Trumpet player Herb Alpert in 1969,
when he disbanded the Tijuana Brass
and quit performing